DK Chess for Kids

Written by Michael Basman

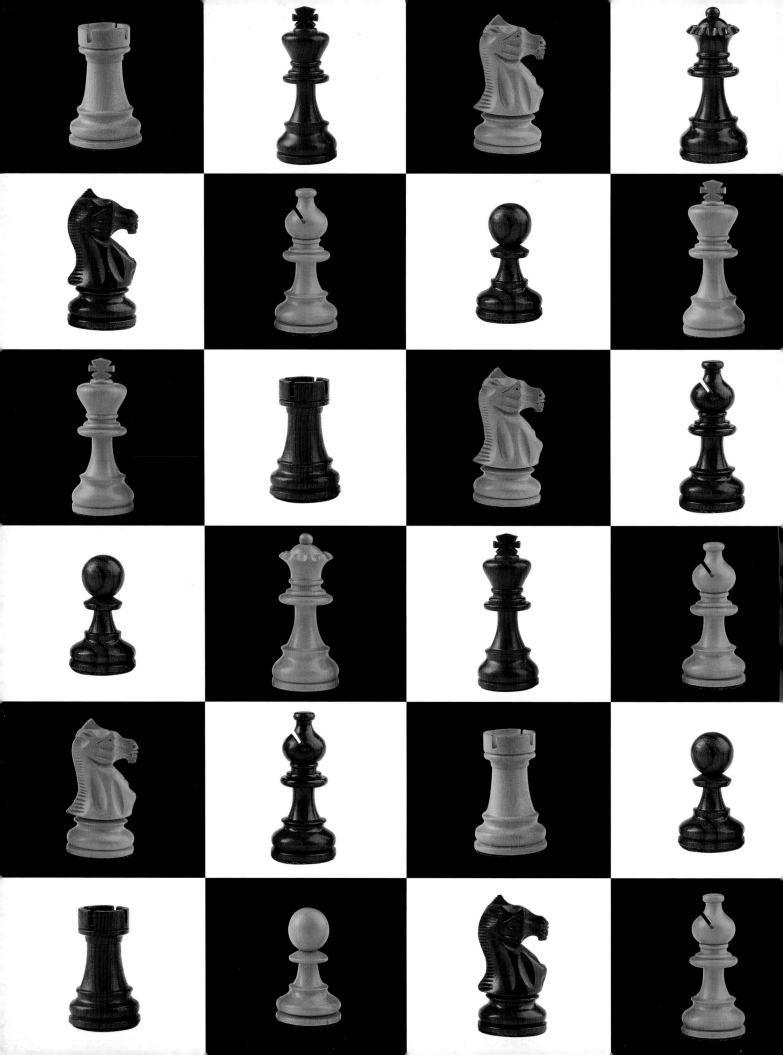

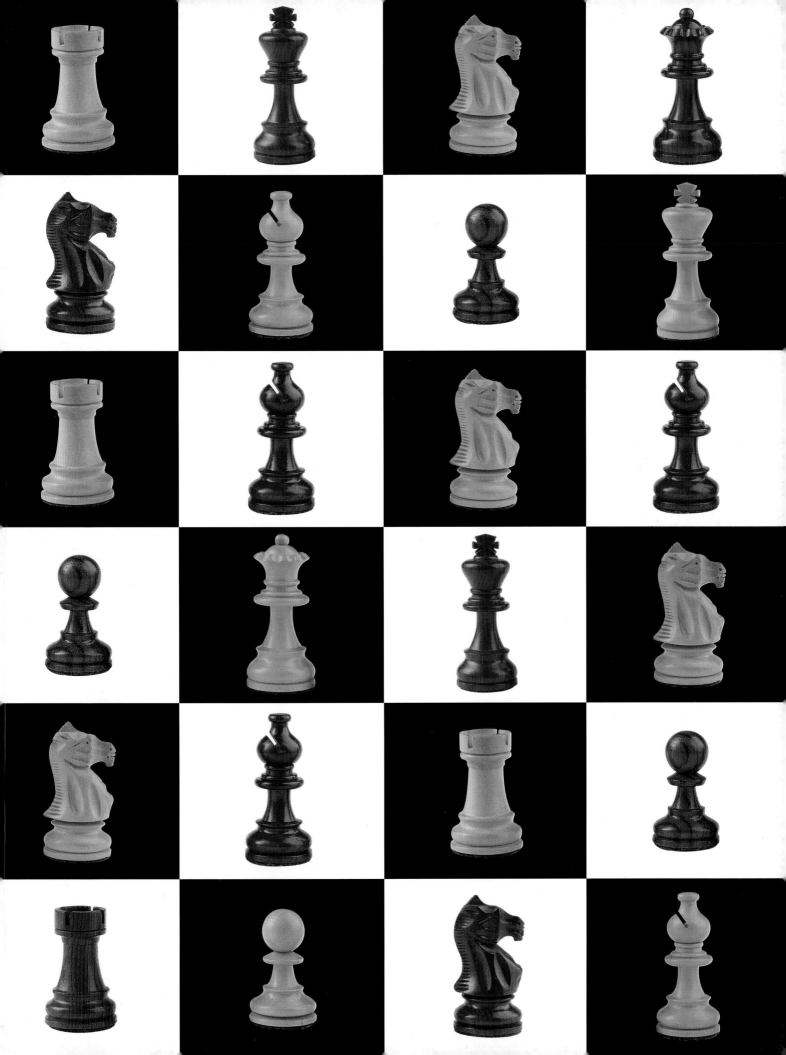

DK Chess for Kids

Written by Michael Basman

LONDON, NEW YORK,
MUNICH, MELBOURNE, and DELHI

Project Editor Elinor Greenwood   **Senior Art Editor** Marcus James
Managing Editor Mary Ling
Managing Art Editor Rachael Foster
Digital Artwork Robin Hunter
Photography Steve Gorton
DTP Designer Almudena Díaz
Picture Researcher Andrea Sadler
Jacket Designer Hedi Gutt
Jacker Editor Mariza O'Keeffe
Production Erica Rosen

Published in the United States by Dorling Kindersley Publishing, Inc.
345 Hudson St. New York, New York 10014

First American hardback edition, 2001
First American paperback edition, 2006

17 26 25 24
037-KC300-Jan/06

Library of Congress Cataloging-in-Publication Data

Paperback edition ISBN-13: 978-0-7566-1807-0   ISBN-10: 0-7566-1807-X
Hardback edition ISBN-13: 978-0-7894-6540-5   ISBN-10: 0-7894-6540-X

Color reproduction by Colourscan, Singapore
Printed and bound in China

See our complete catalog at
www.dk.com

Contents

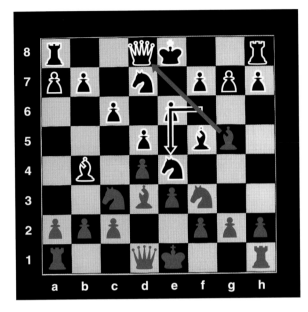

To all young chess players

"**A**LL OVER THE WORLD people are taking up the challenge of chess, meeting new opponents, and testing their mental strength. The power of the mind – the avenue to success in business and study – is awakened, developed, and strengthened by chess. There is no feeling more satisfying than beating an able opponent; and to be a winner you just need confidence, concentration, and the ability to learn – from books, videos, computers, and your own defeats. Chess was once the game of royalty, but is now open to everyone. "

Michael Basman

"I have been playing chess since I was 10 years old, and since then I haven't been away from a chess board for long! Each game I play is still exciting and challenging."

"A jubilant Rosalind Kieran and I. She had just won the Under 9 Suprema at the Daihatsu Kinghams Megafinal of 1992. Seven years later, Rosalind represented England in the World Girls' Championship."

"Since becoming an International Master in 1981, I have devoted my time to teaching chess to schoolchildren. In 1996, I launched the UK Chess Challenge. In its first year it attracted 23,000 players, and now that number has risen to 40,000. In this picture, I am photographed with the category winners."

"Here I am playing chess with a young opponent. I have made many friends through playing chess and enjoy the friendly rivalry the game encourages."

History of chess

CHESS HAS A LONG HISTORY. It is at least 1,500 years old. The oldest pieces to be discovered date from the 6th century AD. Before that, chess might have been played, but nobody can be sure. Chess is certainly a descendant of the Indian game *Chaturanga*, meaning "four sides" – because Indian armies were made up of four parts: the chariots, the cavalry, the elephants, and the infantrymen. The ultimate war game, chess is based on ancient battle scenarios which can still be applied to the game played by people all over the world today.

Chinese chess
A close relation to chess is the Chinese game of *Hsiang Chi* (meaning "elephant game"), which is still very popular in China. The date this game originated is not known.

Chess goes west
The game of chess spread with the opening of markets between East Asia and Persia in the 10th century. Arab merchants plying their way along the famous Silk Road would often have a chess set among their baggage. As a result, travelers and traders eventually introduced chess into Europe.

An explosive growth in interest
Until the late 19th century, chess was known by the nickname "the game of kings" because of its popularity among the upper classes. However, in the 20th century ordinary people started taking up the game by the thousands.

The match of the century
Since 1948, the Russians have ruled supreme in the world of chess. However, American Bobby Fischer, the "boy from Brooklyn," took on the might of the Soviet Union when he beat the reigning World Champion, Boris Spassky, in Reykjavik, Iceland, in July 1972.

Bobby Fischer

Boris Spassky

Women prove themselves
Sofia Polgar – one of the trio of brilliant Polgar sisters

Before the Hungarian Polgar family exploded onto the chess scene, it was a widely held belief that women could not play chess. However, the Polgar sisters – Susan, Sofia, and Judith – proved this wrong. Judith became the world's youngest Grandmaster at 15 years old, beating even the record held by the incredible Bobby Fischer.

Young champions
Chess is a game that children can play just as well as adults. This has been true of chess throughout its history, but it is only now that children are really coming into the limelight. Here Luke McShane, Under 10 World Champion, is practicing his moves.

The chess set

A CHESS SET IS MADE up of 32 pieces and a board. The board acts as a simple battlefield, where there are no trees, rivers, hills, valleys, or buildings to hide behind. This means you can control the events of the battle far better than any army general. The pieces are the opposing armies, and the numbers on both sides are the same, so the game begins on an equal footing. It is how you move your pieces that determines eventual victory – or defeat.

Files are rows that run from one player's end to the other's. Here the edge file is blue.

A diagonal is marked by the red squares.

Ranks are rows across the board. Here the first rank is green.

Your army

Chess pieces come in many shapes and sizes. But the pieces most widely used are the Staunton-pattern pieces, which are the ones used in tournaments and in this book. The two armies are collectively called "the pieces." In your army you have a king, a queen, two bishops, two knights, two rooks, and eight pawns. (Note: sometimes chess players refer to pawns as different to "the pieces," meaning king, queen, bishops, knights, and rooks, though technically they are all "pieces.")

The battlefield

There are special terms for the rows of squares going sideways – these are called the "ranks." There are eight ranks on the chess board. The rows that go vertically, top to bottom, are called "files." There are also eight of these. Lastly, the squares of the same color going in one direction are called "diagonals." Surprisingly enough, there are 26 diagonals on the chess board.

It's black and white
No matter what color the pieces are – red and black, pink and purple – the lighter color is always called "White" and the darker color is always called "Black."

One king
As the head of the army, the king is the tallest piece. Although the most important, he cannot move far and is therefore not powerful. If he cannot avoid capture, he is "checkmated" and the game is over.

One queen
The queen is your most powerful piece. She can attack almost half of the squares on the board from one position. She is both fast and wide-ranging.

Two bishops
Your bishops are recognized by the distinctive "cuts" in their heads – representing bishops' hats. Bishops are agile pieces that move swiftly along the diagonals.

Two knights
These unique pieces are the only ones that can leap over obstacles, and the only ones that don't travel in a straight line. In the often crowded conditions of the chess board, you will find your knights invaluable.

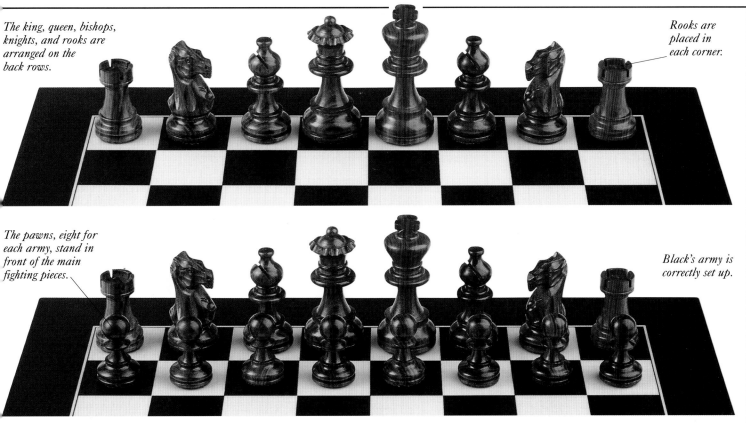

The king, queen, bishops, knights, and rooks are arranged on the back rows.

Rooks are placed in each corner.

The pawns, eight for each army, stand in front of the main fighting pieces.

Black's army is correctly set up.

Setting up the board

First you must place the board between you and your opponent, who sits across from you. A white corner square of the board must always be to the right of each player. Then you place the pieces in their correct positions. The white army and the black army are set up at opposite ends of the board, facing each other. The king and queen are in the middle. Then come the bishops, knights, and rooks spanning out on each side. Finally the pawns are placed on the row in front.

The white queen is placed on a white square, the black queen on a black square.

The king and queen of each army are opposite each other.

Remember! White square on the right.

Two rooks

This pair of sturdy pieces, which use the ranks and files, look like castles and in fact are frequently called "castles." Your rooks are the second most powerful pieces, after the queen, but they are also the hardest to get into the action.

Eight pawns

These are the infantrymen of the chess board, and there are eight in each army. Your pawns often enter the action first. Pawns are the least powerful pieces – but they have ambition. If a pawn reaches the end of the board, it can be promoted, perhaps even to the status of the mighty queen.

The aim of the game

THE AIM OF CHESS, simply, is to trap your opponent's king and deliver "checkmate." Actually doing it, however, isn't so simple. Chess is a battle of wits between two players, each controlling their own army. The battle can last for hours or end very suddenly. You can gain the advantage by steady pressure, building up your attack slowly by capturing enemy pieces, while keeping your own pieces safe. Or a well-aimed blow after only a few moves can end the game.

Developing/capturing

Though checkmate is the aim of the game, you build up to it by weakening the enemy army through capturing pieces. The idea is that your opponent will then be too weak to resist, and will not be able to defend the king. Players must first compete for a good position in the middle of the board. One player will get the upper hand, and will then be able to invade enemy territory, capture weak enemy pieces, or open up a decisive attack on the enemy king.

Battle it out!

Chess is one of the oldest war games in the world. The pieces represent the armies, and the board represents the battlefield. There is a white army and a black army. The two armies move toward each other and then the fight begins. Attacking and defending strategies are played out as though the players are real generals overseeing a real battle. The general with the best strategy and tactics will win the game.

Checkmate

Checkmate comes as a result of the tactics and strategy of one player being superior to that of the other player's. The player who is "checkmated" (or "mated") has lost the game. Only more games can increase your skill and help you learn to be the victor in the next match.

White's general is pleased because she is playing an effective move.

White has captured one knight, one bishop, and one pawn.

Black's general will have to think of a way to improve his position.

Black has captured White's two knights and one pawn.

Simple notation

HOW MANY LANGUAGES do you know? English, probably, maybe some French or German, or some other language. Perhaps you know the language of music, with its whole notes, eighth notes, and staves. Chess has its own language too, but it's much easier to learn. It's a simple way to name the squares and to describe the movement of pieces across the board.

The pieces

Each piece is represented by a symbol in chess diagrams. These are not the same for every book. Although they come in a variety of colors, shapes, and sizes, it's usually easy to tell which symbol stands for what. In notation, each piece is given a letter to make it easy to tell which one you are writing about. You always use capital letters when referring to the pieces.

This is the symbol for the king. In notation a king is written as just "K." Note the symbol is red, although it stands for a white piece and is called "white."

K

This is the symbol for the white queen. In notation a queen is written as just "Q."

Q

This is the white bishop. In notation a bishop is written as just "B."

B

A knight is written as "N." The king took the "K" first!

N

A rook is written as "R."

R

There are so many pawns that it is simpler to note them by their position on the board. The pawn has no letter.

Check it out!

The chess board can be read in the same way as a map. Look at this map. The chess club is in square C1. If you can read a map, you can read a chess board.

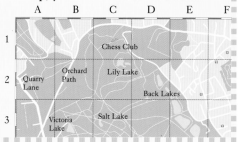

The board

The board is made up of 64 squares, in eight rows of eight squares. If we place the numbers 1 to 8 at the side of the board, and the letters a to h along the bottom of the board, by matching up the numbers and letters we can give every square its own name. The letter comes first, followed by the number. Take a look at the diagram to see how it works.

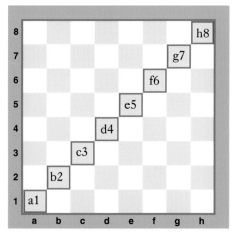

It's your move!

Look at the board. Can you write down where the black rook is? How about the black knight, black king, white queen, white pawn, and white bishop? For example, the white queen is on square c1.

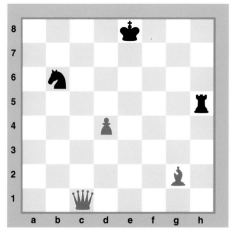

Pawns

THE PIECES ARE RANKED from the highest to the lowest, and nothing is lower than a pawn. In fact its name seems to come from the Old French *paon*, meaning "infantryman." Yet the pawn is a fascinating piece, and many players see it as the soul of chess. What a pawn lacks in strength, it makes up for in numbers. The pawns take the brunt of early fighting, they control territory, and are the king's natural guardians.

Check it out!

In Lewis Carroll's *Alice through the Looking Glass*, many characters are inspired by chess pieces. Alice herself is a white pawn who eventually makes her way to the top of the board where she is promoted to a queen.

Advance!

A player often moves a pawn before anything else, just as a general might send in the infantrymen before the cavalry on a battlefield. On its first move each pawn can move two squares forward, or one square forward. After that it can only move one square forward at a time. Pawns never move backward.

The black pawn has moved only one square forward.

The pawns are lined up like footsoldiers at the start of a battle.

The white pawn has moved two squares forward, because it is its first move

Capturing

Unlike all the other pieces, pawns do not capture in the same way that they move. They move straight forward, but they capture diagonally forward one square.

This pawn moves diagonally forward to capture the knight.

This knight is removed from the board and the white pawn takes its place.

It's your move!

Look at this game position. Which black pieces can white pawns capture? (Answers on page 43.)

14

En passant

En passant means "in passing" in French. In chess it is a rule that prevents a pawn from slipping past an enemy pawn by moving forward two squares on its first move. En passant can happen anytime during a game. A pawn moving up two squares can be captured by an enemy pawn standing next to it. The enemy pawn, capturing diagonally, takes the position of the captured pawn as though it had only moved one square.

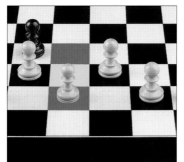

1 This white pawn, on its first move, moves two squares forward.

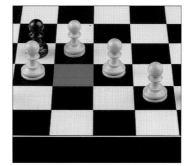

2 It settles alongside an enemy pawn. The pawn has skipped the square the black pawn is diagonally attacking, marked in red.

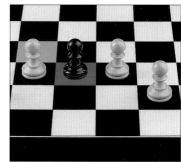

3 Next move, the black pawn can capture the white pawn diagonally, as though it had only moved one square.

Promotion

Pawns have a special feature, which makes them individually precious and often sways the result of a game. A pawn starts the game as the lowest piece, but if it reaches the end of the board – crossing six squares without mishap or capture – it can become a queen, a rook, a bishop, or a knight. The queen is the most powerful piece on the board, so players would usually choose to promote their pawn to a queen. In fact, pawn promotion is often referred to as "queening."

A white pawn has reached the end of the board and become a queen.

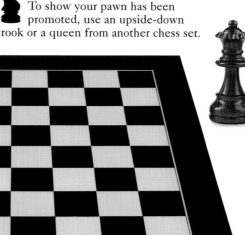

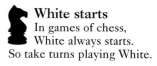

Promoting a pawn
To show your pawn has been promoted, use an upside-down rook or a queen from another chess set.

The queen is the most powerful piece, but you can also promote your pawn to a rook, a bishop, or a knight – it depends on what is the most useful at the time.

The pawn game

Play this game with a friend, using only the pawns. This will give you a firm idea of how pawns move, capture, and promote. The en passant rule also applies, so watch out! The winner is the first to cross the board and promote a pawn. However, if Black can promote a pawn one move after White, the game is a draw (as White starts – the two colors must have the same number of moves). The game is also a draw if both sides cannot move at all. Look at this example game.

White starts
In games of chess, White always starts. So take turns playing White.

1 White has started and moved a pawn up two squares. Black has mirrored its move. Both pawns are now stuck.

2 White has moved a second pawn up two squares. A mistake! It can be taken. Black makes the capture.

3 White moves a pawn up one square, and lays down a challenge to the advancing black pawn. Will Black capture again?

4 Good move! Black moves forward. Now the black pawn cannot be stopped. Black will get a queen in two moves and win the game.

Bishops

BISHOPS ONCE HELD powerful positions as the king's chief advisors, and the king would ask for their blessing before every battle. In chess, the bishops are a formidable pair. Like bishops of old, they are powerful pieces that often work together, one moving along the white diagonals and the other moving along the black diagonals. Between them they can cover all of the squares.

Moving

Bishops only move along the diagonals. They can move backward and forward and are especially effective if they are positioned in the middle of the board. Bishops are blocked if there is a piece in the way as they cannot jump.

Notice how the bishop in the middle of the board controls 13 squares, and the bishop on the edge controls only seven.

The "white-square" bishop is so-called because it only moves along the white diagonals.

The "black-square" bishop only moves along the black diagonals.

Capturing

The bishops capture in the same way as they move: diagonally. The white-square bishop only captures pieces on the white squares, while the black-square bishop only captures on the black squares. Because of their wide range, bishops are useful in guarding long tracts of squares.

The bishop moves along the white diagonal to capture the knight.

The knight is removed from the board to sit out the rest of the game. The bishop takes its place.

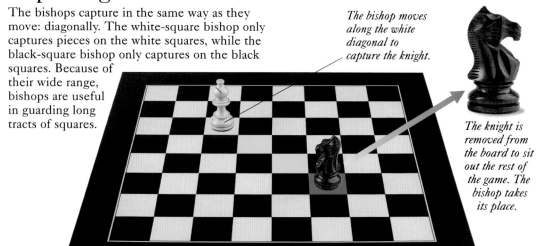

It's your move!

The white bishop can capture all the black pieces in eight moves. Black will kindly keep still for White's rampage. There are two ways of doing this. Can you work them out? (Answer on page 43.)

Knights

MOST OF THE PIECES on the board move in a straightforward way; the rook, queen, bishop, king, and even the pawn are variations on the straight or diagonal move. The knights, however, are governed by completely different rules. They can travel in an L-shape and can also jump over obstacles, just like real horses.

Moving

A knight can jump from one square to another, without touching the ground in between. This means it can jump over other pieces. Yet a knight jumps neither in a straight line nor diagonally. It is best described as an "L-shaped" move. The knight crosses two squares in a straight line, and then goes either one square to the right or one square to the left.

The knight can jump in an L-shape in any direction. It can hit a maximum of eight squares from one position.

Like bishops, knights have more power in the center than on the edge.

Capturing

The knight captures in the same way that it moves. It therefore has a maximum of eight squares that it can attack at any one time. Because it can jump, the knight never gets blocked in, and as a result can really "float like a butterfly and sting like a bee."

This knight jumps in an L-shape onto the square occupied by the black pawn.

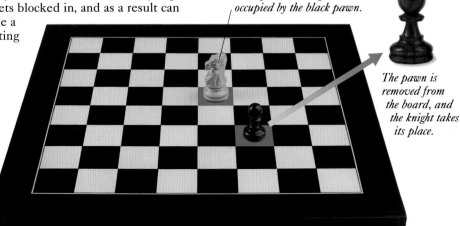

The pawn is removed from the board, and the knight takes its place.

It's your move!

The white knight can capture all the black pieces in six moves. Again, they will kindly stand still. Can you work out the two ways to do it? (Answer on page 43.)

Rooks

THERE ARE TWO ROOKS in each army. At the beginning of a game, they stand at the corners of the board like fortresses guarding the outskirts. Rooks are often the last to enter the fray, but when they do they make very efficient weapons of attack, second only to the queen.

Moving

The rook moves along the ranks and files of the chess board. It can access every square of the board, and at any one time it can control a maximum of 15 squares. A rook cannot jump over any other pieces, except when it makes a special move called "castling" (see page 22). Once your rooks are brought into play, they can cover the board very well.

Chess culture

The rook is shaped like a castle tower. Up until the 15th century, kings lived in castles, where their army could easily defend them. The rook in the chess army defends the king very effectively, as well as being a powerful weapon of attack.

Rooks rarely come into play at the beginning of a game.

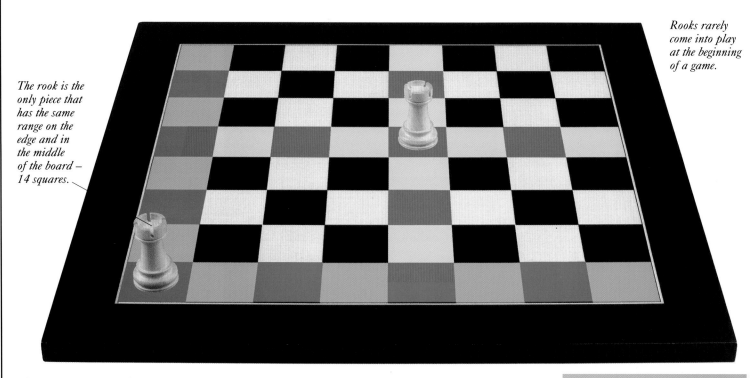

The rook is the only piece that has the same range on the edge and in the middle of the board – 14 squares.

Capturing

Like the other pieces, the rooks capture by occupying the place of an enemy piece. There must be empty squares between the rook and an enemy piece for it to capture as rooks can't jump. Because the rook can cover every square on the board, it is a dangerous attacking piece.

The rook moves along the rank to take the bishop's place.

The bishop is now "dead wood" and is removed from the board.

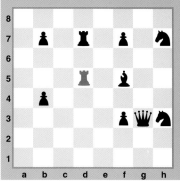

It's your move!

You have nine moves to capture all the black pieces with the white rook. All the white pieces are stuck and cannot move. Can you work out how to do it? (Answer on page 43.)

The queen

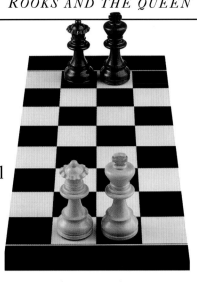

IN THE 15TH CENTURY, the way the queen moved was changed forever. Originally she was one of the weakest pieces, advancing just one square at a time. Once she was given the power to move diagonally and horizontally over all the squares, the game came alive. While the queen stalks the board no piece is safe, and kings tremble behind their stockade of pawns.

Moving

If you've absorbed the moves of the rook and bishop, you will have no trouble understanding the queen as she combines their moves. Your queen can hit a staggering 27 squares from one position, covering both the ranks and files, as well as the diagonals.

The queen moves in every direction. She can move as many squares as she wants, unless she is blocked by another piece. The queen cannot jump.

Queens are "color conscious" at setup. They are placed on the square that matches their color.

Capturing

The queen captures in the same way that she moves. She cannot jump over pieces in the way. Your queen is your most valuable piece, so you must be very careful that she isn't captured. If you lose her, you will find it hard to win against an enemy who still has a queen.

The queen streaks across the board to capture the black knight.

The knight is removed from the board, and the queen takes its place.

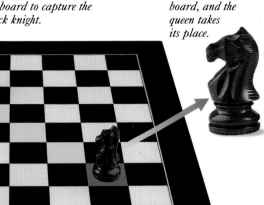

It's your move!

Play this game with a friend. The aim for White is to get one pawn to the other end of the board to be queened. The aim for Black is to prevent this from happening with just one rampaging queen.

The king

THE MOST IMPORTANT piece is the king, although he is by no means the strongest. Unlike the other main pieces, your king can only shuffle along one square at a time. His safety is vital. If your opponent manages to trap your king, so that he cannot avoid capture, the game is over and you have lost. The downfall of the king, as in days of old, means the end for your whole army.

Moving

At any one time your king can move to the eight squares surrounding him, as long as he is not blocked by another piece, nor lands on a square that puts him in check (see page 21). He can move in any direction, but only one square at a time. He is not speedy and cannot make hasty escapes.

The king can move one square in any direction. The squares surrounding him can act as escape routes.

In a game, the king usually stays on the edge of the battlefield, behind a protective wall of pawns.

Capturing

The king captures in the same way that he moves. Don't forget that although he is weak, he can still capture, and this can sometimes get him out of sticky situations.

The knight is removed from the board and the king takes the knight's place.

Here the white king moves diagonally one square to capture a knight.

Check

When the king is attacked by an enemy piece, it is called "check." If your king is in check, your next move has to be to get him out of check. You can do this by moving your king out of trouble, blocking the attack with another piece, or capturing the enemy piece that is threatening you.

The white king is in check from the black bishop. He can escape by moving one square sideways to the right, by capturing the bishop with his rook, or by blocking the attack with his bishop.

Checkmate

"Checkmate" (or "mate" for short) is when the king is under attack and he cannot escape. No matter what move is made, the king can be captured and the game is lost. For this reason every move throughout the game is made with the ultimate aim of checkmate in mind. Checkmating your opponent can be achieved in just two moves, or it can be a long struggle that can take more than 50. Either way, giving checkmate is a thrill – you have won the battle.

Master players can see when a situation is hopeless and resign by knocking over their king before checkmate occurs.

The black queen moves in to deliver a fatal blow.

The white king is in checkmate. There is nowhere for him to go and White has lost the game.

Checkmate challenge

Look at these diagrams. Can you find the move in each one that gives checkmate? You are playing White and it's White's move. (Answers on page 43.)

1 In this diagram, White can give checkmate in one move. The black king cannot move onto the rank covered by the rook on a7. What is the winning move?

2 Here White can give checkmate by moving the bishop on f3. Which square should the bishop move to?

3 Here the black king is vulnerable and the white queen is ready to pounce. Where should she go?

King of the castle

IT IS IMPORTANT to understand the king's relationships with the other pieces. Here we look at "castling," a special rule that moves your king to safety, almost as though he is in a real castle. Once you have learned the attacking strengths of your enemy's pieces, and how your pawns make effective guards, your king should be safe from ambush.

Check it out!
Castles were the only buildings safe enough for kings to live in. The "castling" move is an echo of the past and it is just as effective against attack as a real castle.

Castling

Both sides can tuck their kings into a corner, using a rule called "castling." Castling is the only time you can move two pieces at the same time – the king moves two squares, and the rook jumps over! Castling happens on the back row, behind the pawns. You can only castle if the squares are empty between the king and rook, and the king and rook have not yet moved.

There are spaces between the king and rook, so White is ready to castle. The king moves two squares right...

... and then the rook jumps over.

There are three empty squares so the king moves two spaces to the left...

... and then the rook jumps over.

King's-side castling
This is when your king castles on his own side of the board. If both the knight and bishop have moved out of the way, so there are empty squares between the king and the rook, the king moves two squares toward the rook, and then the rook jumps over.

Queen's-side castling
If the pieces on the queen's side of the board are moved out of the way – the queen, bishop, and knight – so that there are three empty squares between the king and the rook, you can also castle on this side. This is called queen's-side castling.

When you can't castle

There are three important situations when you can't castle: if the king passes through check on his way; if, by castling, you land in check; or when your king is already in check.

Through check
The coast seems clear for White to castle, but it is not. If White castles, the king will pass over a square attacked by Black's queen, and that's not allowed.

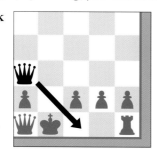

Into check
In this position, White is ready to castle. But the black bishop spoils the party. If White tries to castle, his king will land in check, and that's not allowed either.

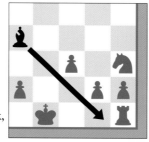

Out of check
The white king would dearly love to castle out of check. It would solve all his problems. Instead he must move, or block the attack with his queen.

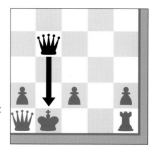

Friend or foe?

The king's best friends are the pawns. Clustered around him at the beginning, they provide protection at all stages of the game. The king also has enemies; your opponent is planning to trap your king and will use every weapon at his or her disposal. The most powerful weapon is the queen. Look at this game, called "Fool's Mate."

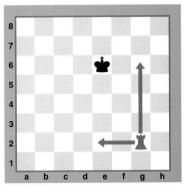

1 White moves a pawn forward two squares. Black also moves a pawn up. Both players have made a conventional opening move.

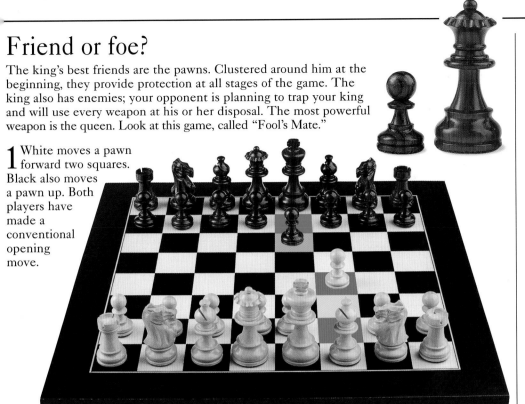

2 White's second pawn moves up, forgetting how important it is to keep the king under guard.

White has moved a pawn to disastrous effect!

3 Black's queen streaks in and delivers checkmate to the powerless white king. The white king has been deserted by his pawns and lost the game in just two moves.

Black's queen delivers checkmate. Game over!

Enemy strength

Try this simple test to measure the strength of enemy pieces. From this you will see why the queen is the most dangerous attacking piece.

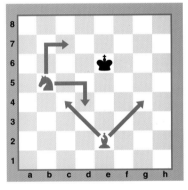

Rook's strength

Put a white rook and a black king on the chess board. You could move the rook to one of two squares, in this diagram g6 and e2, and from both positions the rook could call check.

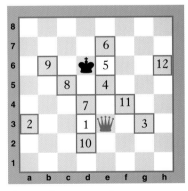

Bishop's and knight's strength

Now put a white knight and a white bishop onto the board. There is a maximum of two squares they can move to that give check for each piece.

Queen's strength

Lastly put a white queen onto the board. From any one position the queen can move to give check from a multitude of squares. In this diagram there are 12 (although squares next to the king are dangerous for her unless she is supported).

Further notation

IT'S TIME TO LEARN a few more of the signs and symbols that will help you to follow the moves in the rest of the book. After a little practice, you'll be able to use what you learn to amaze your friends and family by playing chess without a board or pieces!

Check it out!

Chess notation is like a code. During World War II, top chess players used their familiarity with codes to invent a type of computer that could decode German messages.

This pawn move is written in notation as "a5."

This rook move is written as "Rd7."

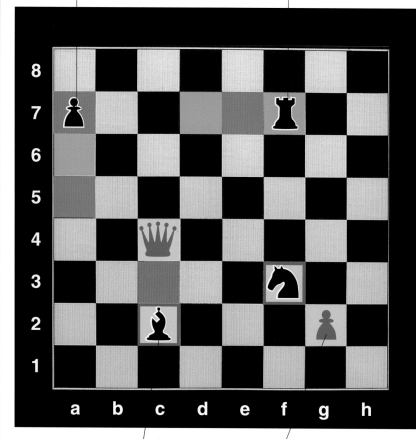

This white queen moving to capture the black bishop is written as "Qxc2."

This white pawn moving to capture the black knight is written as "gxf3."

Moving and capturing

We show how the pieces move by naming the square that they move to.

    Rc2 means "rook moves to square c2."

    e3 means "pawn moves to e3."

You can tell which piece is moving because it is the only one that can move to the named square. The rare cases you can't tell are called "ambiguous moves" (see below). The letter of the piece (always a capital letter) comes before the square it moves to. In the case of the pawn, because it has no letter, you just name the square that it moves to.

Captures are shown by placing an "x" in the middle of a formula:

    Qxb8 means "queen captures at b8."

For pawn captures, you name the file that the pawn came from: *exf4* means "pawn on the e-file captures at f4."

The knights at d7 and g8 can both move to f6.

You write: Ndf6 if the knight on the d-file moves.

You write: Ngf6 if the knight on the g-file moves.

The rooks can both move to a4.

You write: R6a4 if this rook moves because it is on the sixth rank.

You write: R2a4, if this rook moves because it is on the second rank.

Ambiguous moves

Sometimes two of the same pieces of the same color can go to the same square. This usually happens with rooks and knights. To identify which piece moves, you specify where the moving piece came from, i.e. which rank or file, as well as naming the square it moves to.

Following a game

Practice your notation skills by following this game on your chess board. Set up your board in the start position. Read the notation and make the moves, three moves at a time. Notice the way the games are written with each move numbered, and separate columns for White's moves and Black's moves. This game is a famous one, called "Boden's mate," played in London in 1853.

Make a record!
When you're playing a game, practice notation by writing down your moves on a piece of paper as you go along.

	White	Black
1.	e4	e5
2.	Nf3	d6
3.	c3	f5

White's moves *Black's moves*

1 Remember that pawns have no letter, so they are indicated by the position they move to. Also that "N" means one of the knights.

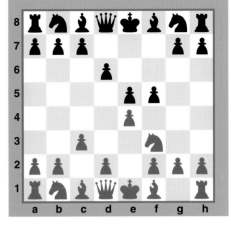

	White	Black
4.	Bc4	Nf6
5.	d4	fxe4
6.	dxe5	exf3

2 Now one of White's bishops has moved into the game. And there have been some neat pawn captures. Both players are jockeying for position.

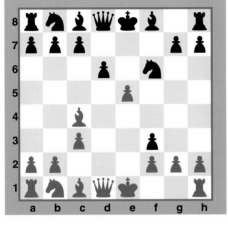

	White	Black
7.	exf6	Qxf6
8.	gxf3	Nc6
9.	f4	Bd7

3 Black's powerful queen has entered the fray and has already made her presence felt.

	White	Black
10.	Be3	0-0-0
11.	Nd2	Re8
12.	Qf3	Bf5

4 Following so far? Good. See how neatly the black king was tucked away when Black castled on the queen's side. White is looking a little vulnerable.

	White	Black
13.	0-0-0	d5
14.	Bxd5	Qxc3+
15.	bxc3	Ba3++

5 Black seemed foolish to lose the queen. But Black had a good plan... White is beaten by Black's bishops. Checkmate!

It's your move!

Try these two exercises, and find out if you're a natural code-breaker. (Answers on page 43.)

1 Look at the four moves made by White in this diagram and write them down in chess notation on a piece of paper.

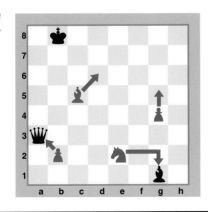

2 Crack the codes for this short game and do the moves on your chess set. You should end up with the checkmate position shown here. This is called "Scholar's mate."

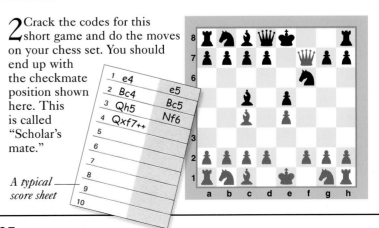

	White	Black
1	e4	e5
2	Bc4	Bc5
3	Qh5	Nf6
4	Qxf7++	
5		
6		
7		
8		
9		
10		

A typical score sheet

Opening

IF YOU HAVE FOLLOWED everything so far, you are equipped with enough knowledge to play a game. You can move your pieces around the board, capture enemy pieces, and maybe even get checkmate. However, to play well you will need to understand the second half of this book, starting with the first phase of a chess game – called the "opening." There are more books written on the opening than on any other part of the game, and over nine million possible positions after only three moves. Do you have to learn all these positions by heart? No. With just a few ideas you can play the opening very well.

Starting your game sets the scene for the battle ahead. If you play a good opening, you will have a good basis for attack later in the game.

Five opening rules

If you decide your opening moves based on the following five rules, you will get off to an excellent start. These rules are relevant to all chess players, whether you are a beginner or a Grandmaster. They are simple and easy to follow. Keep in mind that opening play is about gaining a strong position on the board from which to launch your attack, not for embarking on an immediate onslaught.

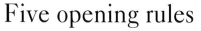

Light brigade

In the first stage of the opening, only the pawns, bishops, and knights should be brought into play. This "light brigade" is used for initial skirmishes and for gaining a good central position. The more valuable queen and rooks make up the "heavy brigade" (see pages 28-29).

Both sides' light brigades have been mobilized to take up good central positions.

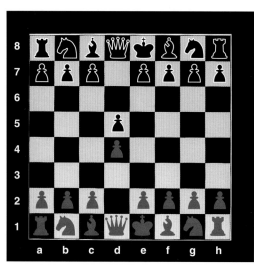

1 Pawns in the center

Place one or two pawns in the center. The center of the board is where the first power struggle takes place, and whoever controls more of the midfield controls the game. Once the pawns have taken up position in the midfield, it's quite hard to dislodge them, so they may stay there for a long time.

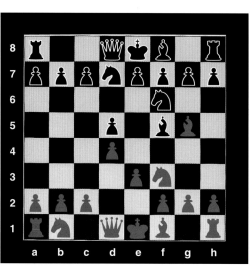

2 Knights and bishops in the center

This is an important rule. Send your knights and bishops into the center. This will mean moving pawns to clear the path of your bishops, which can't jump. Knights, bishops, and pawns are your "light brigade" and need to be moved before your queen and rooks – the "heavy brigade."

3 Move each piece once

As we have seen, the opening is about putting your pieces into good positions near the center, ready for action. Your attacks come later. If you move the same piece around, making attacks, you'll soon end up with one piece fighting an entire army. Instead, move each piece once.

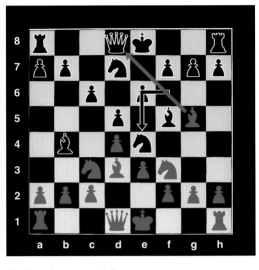

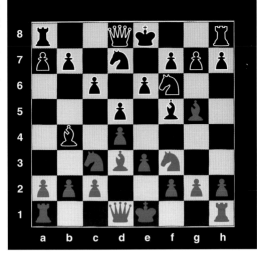

4 Guard and capture

Be careful with the placing of your pieces. If your opponent can capture, make sure you can recapture so the armies stay level. Here Black has made a mistake. Moving the knight to e4 means that White can capture the queen!

5 Castle your king

Make your king safe by castling early. Castling removes your king from the center and puts him on the edge, behind a stockade of pawns. In this picture the game has continued as though Black hasn't lost the queen. When you are playing, you should aim for an opening position like this.

Look and learn
If you take opportunities to watch or study real chess games, you will find it easier to become a good player yourself.

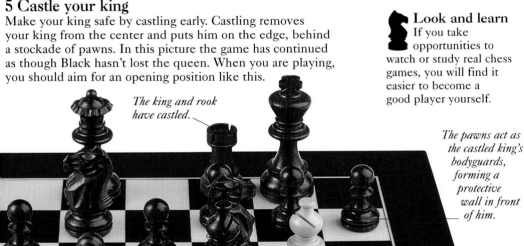

The king and rook have castled.

The pawns act as the castled king's bodyguards, forming a protective wall in front of him.

It's your move!

Before you play your first game of chess using the new opening rules, test yourself on these positions. Are you on the right lines? Choose the best move out of the three options. In all these positions you are playing White. (Answers on page 43.)

1 Choose a move!
a. Pawn to e4
b. Pawn to h4
c. Knight to h3

Choose a move!
2 a. Bishop to b5
b. Knight to a3
c. Pawn to d3

3 Choose a move!
a. Knight to f3
b. Pawn to e5
c. Knight to c3

The major pieces

BY FOLLOWING THE FIVE RULES of the opening, you are already getting off to a good start. But so far we have not looked at bringing the major pieces into play – your queen and rooks. They make up the "heavy brigade" and are extremely powerful and valuable pieces; a lot like owning two tanks and a rocket launcher. With these weapons you can do immense damage to the enemy position. However, you do need to be careful with them. You need a plan of action that will put them into strong positions without exposing them to danger.

The heavy brigade

Unlike the "light brigade" (the pawns, knights, and bishops) the "heavy brigade" (queens and rooks) should not be placed in the center right away. You must deploy them farther back, and always keep in mind "minimum exposure, maximum power."

The queens in both armies move off the back rows to well-covered squares at the rear.

Minimum exposure

Your major pieces are important to your eventual victory, so you must be very careful with them. The queen and rooks should fire at the enemy from a distance, at the rear of the field, where enemy units cannot easily attack them. It's a good idea to move your queen off the back rank, bringing her into play and freeing up the back row for the rooks to move along.

The rooks are free to move to open or half-open files.

Open and half-open files

Pawns need to be cleared out of the way to get the rooks into the action. An "open" file has pawns on it. A "half-open" file has pawns of one color on it.

Maximum power

Clearing the way for your rooks is your priority at this stage (maximum power). Castling is a good way to get your rooks out of the corner, as well as to protect your king. Then, if you can move your rooks to an open or half-open file, so much the better. Your idea should be to have both the rooks and the queen in strong positions but not too far forward.

The white rook moves across to a half-open file.

This file is open. White's other rook can move here next move.

An opening

Now we will follow the course of an opening, and show how the rooks and the queen are brought into play, keeping in mind "minimum exposure, maximum power." Make all the moves on your chess board.

1.	e4	c5	
2.	Nf3	d6	
3.	Bb5+	Bd7	
4.	Bxd7+	Nxd7	
5.	0-0	Ngf6	

1 Five moves have been made. The two sides have exchanged bishops and advanced their light brigades. A good central position is the aim for both players.

7.	...	cxd4

Interrupted notation
"..." shows that White has already moved. For example, in step 2, White's seventh move was d4 (see above). Black's following seventh move is preceded by "..." to show that White has already moved.

3 Black has acted as expected and has captured White's pawn. White will of course immediately recapture with the knight on f3. Black's c-file and White's d-file have now been opened.

10.	Qe2	Rc8
11.	Rad1	

The light brigades are in good central positions, and the heavy brigades have been deployed well by both sides.

5 White moves the queen off the back row, and both Black and White move their rooks onto half-open files.

6.	Nc3	g6
7.	d4	

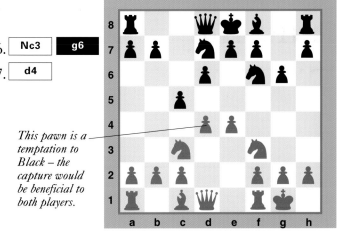

This pawn is a temptation to Black – the capture would be beneficial to both players.

2 White is now offering an exchange to Black. Black can capture White's pawn at d4 and White can recapture with the knight on f3. It would be to both players' advantage to create open files for later deployment of their rooks.

8.	Nxd4	Bg7
9.	Be3	0-0

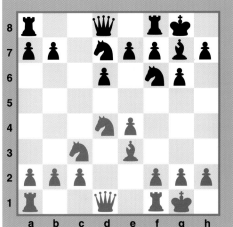

The white king is tucked away in a corner.

4 Next, both players move their bishops off the back rows, following the five rules of the opening as well as clearing space for the rooks behind them. White remembers the important opening rule of castling early.

11.	...	a6
12.	f4	Qc7

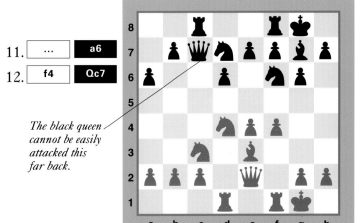

The black queen cannot be easily attacked this far back.

6 The black queen is also moved off the back row to a safe position at the rear. Both generals have directed their armies well and kept to the rules of the opening. It's still anyone's game.

Essential techniques

WE CAN DREAM of being a pop star, a famous actor, or a football hero, but behind any success there are months of preparation, practice, and setbacks. To be a champion chess player takes the same kind of dedication, and the foundations of your success will be your ability to learn basic attacking and defending techniques. We are now moving into the important "middlegame" phase of a chess game, and start by introducing piece value.

Value

There is a value system that you can use to guide you. Your pawns are worth one point each, your knights and bishops are worth three points each, your rooks are worth five points, and your queen is worth a grand total of nine points. Your king, of course, is priceless.

1   3   3   5   9

Taking the black queen is an excellent capture for White, worth nine points!

Capturing the black bishop will give White a reasonable three points, but capturing the queen is much better.

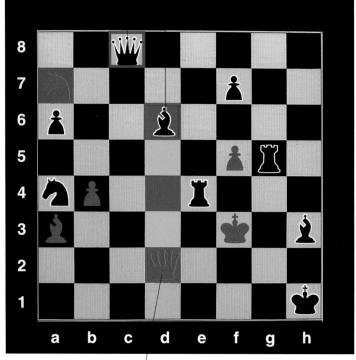

White's queen can capture Black's bishop, but always study the board to see if there are any better captures you can make.

Capturing and value

Capturing is a very precise skill. At every move you should be working out all the possible captures you can make and rank them in order of their points value. The best captures are the ones that win the most points. On this board (left) White can make two captures: Nxc8 and Qxd6. Nxc8 is the best capture because the black queen is worth nine points. Capturing the bishop would only gain White three points. Capturing your opponent's strong pieces, while holding onto your own, is a sure way to eventual victory.

Here the white bishop captures the black rook and is recaptured by Black's queen. White has gained two points, as a rook is worth two points more than a bishop.

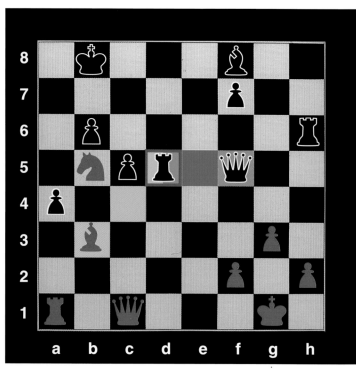

Recapture

In a game of chess, many pieces that you may want to attack are defended. You can capture an enemy piece, only to find that you are then captured back. This is called "recapture." In a game you must decide who gains or loses after a capture and recapture. You do this by measuring how many points, according to the value system, have been "exchanged." So if your bishop takes a pawn and is then recaptured, you have got the worst of the bargain. You deduct one point for the pawn from the three points for the bishop and find that your opponent has won two points. It's simple math!

The blue squares are completely safe for White to move to. The other squares on the board are all attacked by Black.

Nc5 is safe-enough. The knight could be captured by the black rook on c8, but Black dare not capture as he would lose points when White then recaptures with the pawn on b4.

Qh6 is also a safe-enough move. True, Black could play Qxh6, but White could then recapture, Bxh6, and the points would be level.

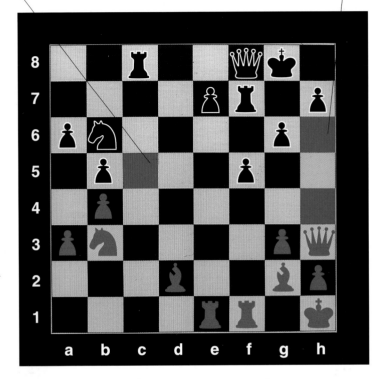

Safe move

Moving your pieces around the chess board is like walking through a minefield. However, there is one big difference. None of the mines on the chess board are hidden. You can scan the board and see just which squares are under attack. Therefore, before you make a move, make sure you have checked that the square you are about to land on is safe. In this picture (above) there are only a few squares that White can move to that are entirely safe.

Mental checklist
Before you move, run through these questions in your head.
1. What is your best move/best capture?
2. By moving a piece, are you leaving any other piece undefended?
3. Are any of your pieces about to be captured?
4. If so, what can you do to defend yourself?

Safe-enough move

The farther you advance into enemy territory, the more you find the squares are guarded by enemy pieces. However, you can still advance your pieces into good positions, provided they are adequately defended by their comrades. Therefore an important technique to master is the safe-enough move. This is where you move to a square attacked by an enemy piece, but you can recapture on that square and do not lose points overall as a result.

It's your move!

Look at each of these diagrams and work out the moves. (Answers on page 43.)

1 How many captures can White make? Write each one down and rank them according to how many points you could gain from each capture. Which is the best capture?

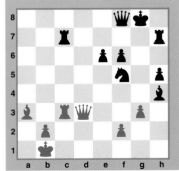

2 What captures can White make? There are four possibilities. Which is the best capture assuming that Black will recapture if he can?

3 Write down the nine moves that are entirely safe for White (moving to squares that the enemy does not attack at all). Well done if you find all nine!

4 White can make the following moves: Rd4, Bxc7, Rd7, and Be5. Which moves are safe, not safe, or safe-enough?

Attack and defend

MAKING PRECISE ATTACKS on enemy pieces is part of your technique. However, half of the moves in a chess game are made by your opponent, so knowing how to defend your pieces is also important. Chess is like a dance, except the idea is to step on your opponent's toes as often as possible, while keeping your own feet out of danger.

Keeping time

In tournaments players are given 2-3 minutes on average to play each move. They are timed by a special clock with two faces. After making a move, a player hits the nearest button on top of the clock. The other clock then starts timing the other player.

Making threats

A simple threat is an attack on an undefended enemy piece or a piece of higher value. Threats force your opponent to waste moves in avoiding attack and help you to establish a strong position. If your threats result in captures, you will gain a stronger army, but any threats you make must be safe or safe-enough moves.

An effective threat

On this board (right), White moves a bishop up to threaten the black knight at d6. This is a safe-enough move, because although the bishop can be captured by Black's queen, White could recapture with the knight on d3 and Black would lose the queen. Black must think of some other way to avoid the danger.

Bb4 is a safe-enough move, which makes an effective threat against Black's knight at d6.

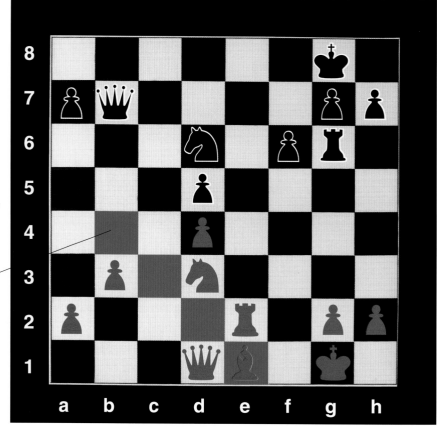

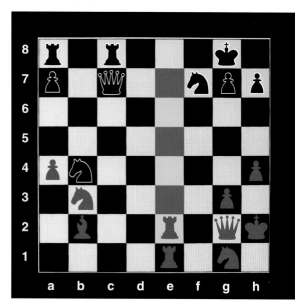

Rooks working in pairs

The rook-to-e7 move makes a threat – against Black's queen at c7. True, the queen can capture White's rook, but White is happy with that deal because the rook is guarded by White's other rook on e1. This is a very effective way to use your rooks.

It's your move!

Improve your attacking skills by making threats on enemy pieces. You are White and it's White's move.

(Answers on page 43.)

1 Mobilize your troops to make an attack! Remember that all threats must be safe or safe-enough moves.

2 There are six possible threats in this position. Can you find them all?

Defending against threats

While you are making good moves, and making threats, your opponent will be doing the same. To avoid enemy threats, there are five main methods of defense, which all resemble defense against physical attack. Look at the positioning on the five chess diagrams. Black's rook at f7 is attacking the white rook at f3. Each diagram shows a different defensive technique.

Defensive moves
1. Move away..........................Run!
2. Capture the enemy............Fight back!
3. Support your piece............Get some friends to help!
4. Block the attack................Use a shield!
5. Counterattack....................Cause a diversion!

1. Move away
In this diagram, White can reduce the threat from Black's rook at f7 by moving the threatened rook to any of the three squares shown.

Rf4
Rf6
Rg3

2. Capture the enemy
White's rook can, of course, capture the black rook – it will be recaptured, but it's an equal exchange.

Rxf7

3. Support your piece
White can defend the rook by moving a bishop to e2. If the black rook carries out its threat, White can recapture.

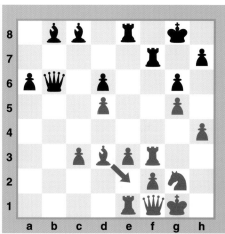

Be2

4. Block the attack
Here White chooses to move a knight in front of the threatened rook to block the attack from Black's rook.

Nf4

5. Counterattack
Here White's other rook moves to threaten Black's queen. This tactic means that White doesn't waste a move, and it throws a wrench in the works. A counterattack only works well if you attack a piece of equal or greater worth.

Rb1

It's your move!
Look at the diagrams and work out all the possible defensive moves that White can make. (Answers on page 43.)

1 Black's queen is threatening White's knight at h3. What defensive moves can White make against the attack?

2 Black's bishop is threatening White's queen at e3. What moves can White make to avoid losing the queen?

Tactics

T HE FOUNDATION OF YOUR success will be the techniques you have already learned. However, you can often speed up the winning process if you gain a knowledge of tactics. Between strong and equally matched players, tactical ability will turn the game one way or another. The main tactical ideas are the fork, the pin, and the discovered attack.

Knight forks

The greatest fork moves of all are made by your knight, which can threaten eight pieces at the same time. In this diagram, the knight can move to c7 and put three pieces under attack.

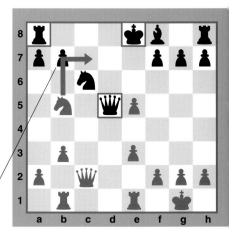

This knight, by moving to c7, makes a devastating fork, attacking the black king at e8, the rook at a8, and the queen at d5.

The fork

The fork is a tactical move where one piece attacks two or more pieces at the same time. This effective tactic makes it very difficult for your opponent to escape with all pieces unscathed, and usually results in a capture. Every single piece on the chess board can fork – even the humble pawn.

The white pawn forks both black rooks. Though one rook can escape in the next move, the other will be captured.

Discovered attack

After torturing your opponent with forks and pins, you can also drop in a few discovered attacks. On the chess board nothing is hidden – all the pieces and all the squares are in full view. The only thing you cannot know is the future and the thoughts in your opponent's head. The discovered attack is the nearest thing you can get to concealment since you do one thing, but threaten another. Look at this example taken from a recent junior game.

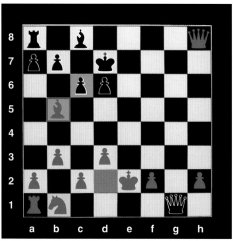

Black's pawn captures White's bishop.

1 Both sides have been going tooth and nail at each other, and now, during a lull in the action, White decides to bring out a knight to d2. Thinking little of it, Black continues with his plan to capture the white bishop at b5 with a pawn.

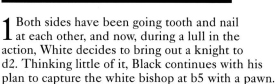

White's rook moves to capture Black's queen.

2 Now the true point of White's plan is revealed – the white rook at a1 captures Black's queen! White's tactical play has paid off and put his army at a massive advantage.

The pin

A pin is another effective tactic. It is an attack on a piece which, if it tries to move, leaves a more valuable piece open to capture. Sometimes this leads to complete paralysis of an enemy piece, sometimes to material gain. With this tactical weapon you can really drive a stake into the heart of your opponent's position.

A pawn is guarding the knight.

This bishop is pinning the white knight to the king.

The knight cannot move or the king will be in check.

A pinned pawn

Here the pinned black pawn at d5 can't be guarded, can't move, and White will capture it on the next move with the bishop at b3. Not only will Black lose a pawn, but Black's king will also be in check.

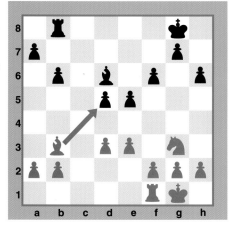

Under pressure

Here the pinned piece – the black knight at c6 – is securely defended by a bishop at b7. But White attacks the knight again with a pawn, moving from d4 to d5. Now Black stands to lose a knight.

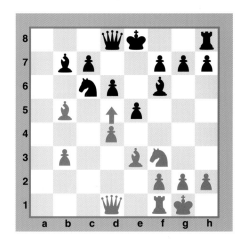

A killer blow

A discovered attack can be even more deadly if you can get the piece that moves to do some attacking work. Look at this situation. Black's pawn moves forward and Black delivers check with a discovered attack from the bishop. White has to escape check and cannot react to the threat posed to the queen by the black pawn. Next move White will lose the queen.

White will have to move to get out of check.

The black pawn will then capture White's queen.

Endgame

W E HAVE SEEN HOW games can end after only a few moves with a neat checkmate. But many games do not finish like that. In fact, though your opponent may be several pieces behind, it is certainly possible to avoid checkmate for a very long time. The term used to describe the end of chess games, when there are only a few pieces left, is "endgame." There are particular skills that you need to play effectively in endgame situations.

Endgame strategy

Good endgame play is the mark of a true master. Working out how to win without many pieces means that you will have to adopt a whole new strategy. Use the three golden rules in the box below.

Black's pawn at a7 has been "mopped up."

1 Look at this endgame. White is way ahead on points but is not going to be able to checkmate quickly, in particular because both queens are off the board. White starts by "swapping down." White's bishop takes the knight at c6, whi will be recaptured by Black's pawn on b7. Follow the notatio below on your chess board to find out the rest of White's plan

1.	Bxc6	bxc6
2.	Re7+	Kf6
3.	Rxa7	d5
4.	a4	

2 White has "swapped down," "mopped up," and with the move to a4 is now well on the way to "queening a pawn." It won't be long before White delivers checkmate.

Golden rules

1. Mop up
Use your extra pieces to clean up remaining enemy pieces.

2. Swap down
Exchange your pieces with enemy pieces until your opponent has virtually nothing left except king and pawns, and you still have fighting units.

3. Queen a pawn
Get a pawn to the end of the board. A new queen will make your checkmating task easy.

It's your move!

Look at these two diagrams. Using the three golden rules – "mop up," "swap down," and "queen a pawn" – choose the correct moves to make in these endgame situations. (Answers on page 43.)

1 Which is the best move for White? Ng6+ or Bd7?

2 Should the white rook on d2 capture the black rook on d6 and then be recaptured? Or should White move the rook out of harm's way?

The lawn mower

We still haven't shown how to actually get checkmate with only a few pieces. The "lawn mower" makes a great weapon with which to crush your poor opponent. One army has two rooks and a king, against one king. Using the rooks as a team, it is possible to get checkmate very quickly.

1.	...
	Rg4

1 Set up your pieces in the position shown in this picture and follow the moves on your board using the notation. Knowing that it would be difficult to give checkmate when the king is in the middle of the board, Black sets to driving the white king to the edge.

2.	Kc3	Rh7
3.	Kd3	Rh3+

2 Black gradually pushes the white king toward the edge. He is now stuck to the back three ranks of the board and will have to retreat further.

4.	Ke2	Rg2+
5.	Kf1	

3 The king is at last at the edge of the field and, by attacking the black rook, threatens to escape. But the slow-footed king is no match for the speedy rooks, who simply transfer themselves to the other side of the field.

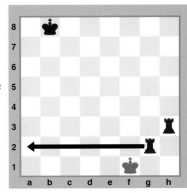

5.	...	Ra2
6.	Kg1	Rb3
7.	Kf1	Rb1++

4 Black's rook moves forward to b1 to give checkmate. The rooks have worked together to great effect. Study this checkmate carefully. It is called the "lawn mower" because the action of the rooks looks like someone mowing a lawn.

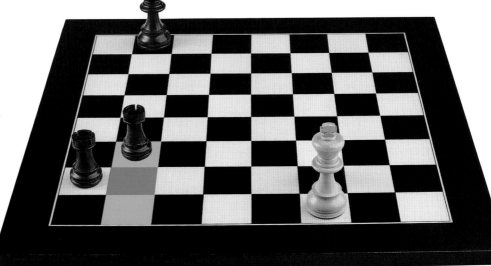

Other checkmates

It may be that you have even fewer pieces at your disposal. In fact with a king and a queen, or a king and a rook, you can still checkmate provided you use your king.

Queen mate

Here, White's king has played a vital role in the attack. Not only has he helped drive the black king to the edge, but also guards the queen as she delivers the kiss of death.

Box mate

This is called "Box mate" because the king and the rook work even more closely together than in Queen mate, and they gradually box in the enemy king.

It's a draw!

SOMETIMES PLAYERS are so evenly matched that neither side is able to win and the game is a draw. There are several ways a game can be drawn, such as when neither player has enough strong pieces left, or a draw by agreement, when neither player can see a way to win. However, there are three other draws set out by the rule book. These are stalemate, a draw by repetition, and the 50-move rule.

Check it out!

In the 1993 World Championship match between reigning champion Gary Kasparov of Russia and Nigel Short of Great Britain, Kasparov was on the brink of defeat in two vital games. However, to stave off disaster, and to keep his championship title, he played a brilliant defense to get a draw in both games.

Stalemate

If a player cannot move any pieces, and his or her king, which is not in check, cannot move anywhere, the position is called a draw by stalemate. Here the black king cannot move except into check. He is not in check now so this game is a stalemate.

This is the best position that White can achieve with just a bishop and a king against a king. It is impossible to get checkmate.

Not enough material

A situation may arise where you simply don't have enough strong pieces left to give checkmate. If only the two kings remain, they cannot checkmate each other. Likewise, you cannot give checkmate with only a bishop and king, or a knight and a king left. Without enough material a game results in a draw.

Forcing a stalemate

Sometimes it is worth intentionally bringing about a draw by stalemate, rather than losing. Here White, about to be checkmated, finds a sly way to draw.

The white rook moves across the board and puts the black king into check. Black is forced to capture the rook with the queen.

On the next move, White can't move any white pieces. The white king cannot move into check. Stalemate!

It's your move!

This is tricky! It is in White's interests to get a draw, otherwise Black will soon deliver checkmate. What move can White make with the rook on g6 to ensure that the result is a draw? Hint: disregard the queen. (Answer on page 43.)

Draw by repetition

If a position repeats itself three times, the game can be declared a draw. If one player keeps checking the other with no escape and no checkmate either, this is known as perpetual check. Look at this series of moves.

1 Black is in a bad postion. White has more points and two strong attacking pieces. Black decides to go for a draw by perpetual check. The black queen moves up to put the white king into check.

The white king is forced to move to the only safe square.

2 White has no other option but to hastily move the king onto the edge to avoid check. However, the white king is not safe yet.

The third draw

The third kind of draw in the chess rule book happens when no pawns have been moved and no captures have taken place for 50 moves. As you can imagine, this doesn't happen very often.

3 Black moves along the diagonal to deliver check again. The white king has nowhere to go unless he moves back to where he came from. The black queen will then move back to where she came from, putting the white king in check again. These moves could continue forever and the result of this game is a draw by perpetual check.

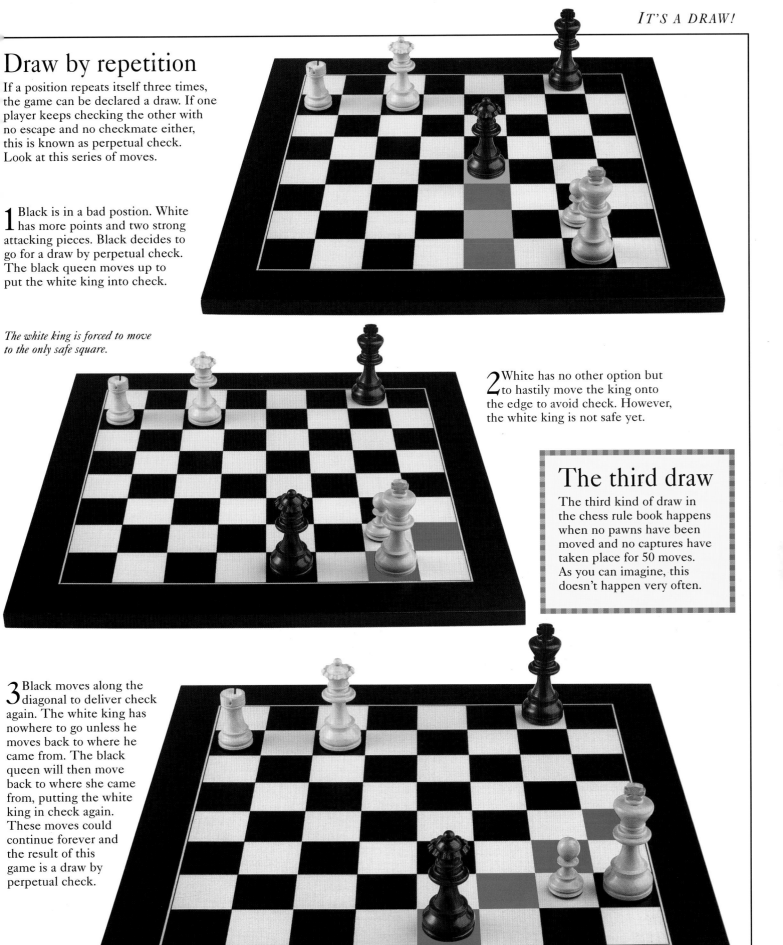

Taking it farther

YOU CAN ENJOY CHESS throughout your life, and it is up to you how you choose to play. Whether you prefer relaxing games with your friends at home or playing hard battles in tournaments, joining a chess club gets you off to a good start. The more you play, whether at a chess club, internet chess, against a computer, or in tournaments, the better you will be. So get out your chess board and pieces and start playing!

These children are playing a game at a school chess club meeting.

Chess clubs

At chess clubs you can practice your skills and techniques against a variety of opponents, as well as get advice from a teacher. Some clubs may invite famous players to come and give talks and demonstrate their skills. Joining a school chess club has been the start for many top chess players, including me! If you get onto a school team, you can go to other schools to play matches. Any games, against as many different people as possible, will help your ability.

Tournaments

Entering a chess tournament means playing in more formal surroundings. At a tournament, you're not allowed any help from other people and your moves are timed. In this photograph (left), the two nearest boys are playing for prize money in the biggest chess tournament in the world – the UK Chess Challenge.

The Mind Sports Olympiad

The Mind Sports Olympiad is the Olympics for all games that require mental agility. There are hundreds of games events, including backgammon, bridge, memory games, and speed-reading tests. Chess is an important part of the agenda. The Olympiad is held annually in London and anyone, from any country, can enter. Gold, silver, and bronze medals are awarded to the top juniors and top adults in each event.

World Championships

Gary Kasparov is regarded as the world's best player, and he has proven his status as World Champion in many championship events. FIDE (the International Chess Federation) currently organizes an annual World Championship match, but with so much chess being played all over the world, other events have been introduced, including a Junior World Championships for girls and boys. The internet is another exciting factor, and an Internet Schools World Championships has been set up by Kasparov which happened for the first time in 2000.

Any challenge to the World Champion is played in the very strictest conditions, in the presence of an arbiter.

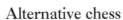

Kasparov and Karpov, shown here, were rivals for the title for eight years.

These people have dressed up as chess pieces and arranged themselves on a big outdoor board.

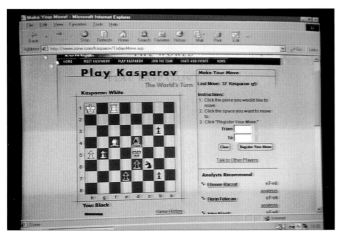

Alternative chess

Chess doesn't have to be played indoors. Some people like to play chess outdoors, in a park, or on a huge outdoor chess set. The people in this picture are playing "human chess" and are dressed up like the pieces to provide a real show. You can play chess in the park, on a train, in the car, outdoors, indoors... wherever you like!

You can set the level that you want to play at according to your ability.

Chess computers

Chess computers come in many shapes and sizes, from "Deep Blue," a computer designed to beat Gary Kasparov, to the ones shown here. These small computers are cheap and useful and can make tremendous opponents.

Chess on the internet

The internet is a great resource for chess players. There are many websites to choose from, and you can find opponents to play against all over the world. The page shown here is the groundbreaking "World against Kasparov" website, on which the whole world had the chance to vote on each move in a game against Kasparov. The game ended in a win for Kasparov.

You enter your move in notation, and then the computer replies with its move. You move the pieces on the board yourself.

Glossary

During practice, or when watching a game, you may find it helpful to understand some of the following words and phrases.

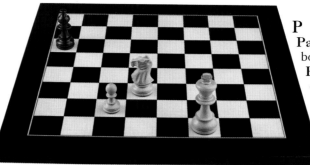

B
Bishop A piece that only moves in a diagonal direction. Each army contains two bishops.

C
Capture When one piece takes an enemy piece. The capturing piece moves onto the square of the enemy piece, which is removed from the board.

Castling A special combined move where the king moves two squares toward a rook and the rook jumps over to stand next to the king.

Check An attack on a king.

Checkmate A situation in which a king is in check and cannot escape – therefore the end of the game.

Chess clock A double clock that measures the time taken by each player to make a move so that the game doesn't last too long.

D
Development Moving the pieces off the back row into a more central position in order to attack.

Diagonal The corner to far corner direction on the chess board.

Diagram A picture of a chess board with the chess pieces in place used to demonstrate specific positions.

Double attack *See* Fork.

Draw A game that cannot be won by either side.

E
Endgame The final phase of the game when only a few pieces are left.

En passant A move where a pawn that has moved up two squares on its initial move in the game can be captured by an enemy pawn standing alongside, as though the pawn had only moved one square.

Exchange A swap or trade of pieces.

F
File A straight row of squares going vertically – ie. from one player to the other.

Fool's mate The shortest possible game ending in checkmate.

Fork When one piece attacks more than one enemy piece at the same time.

H
Half-open file A file with a pawn or pawns of only one color on it.

I
Illegal move A move that breaks the rules of chess.

International Grandmaster A rank above the International Master. One of the strongest players in the world.

International Master A title for a chess player, internationally recognizing a player of great strength.

K
King The most important piece in the game. The whole aim of the game is to capture the enemy king.

King's side The files that are nearest the king – the f-, g-, and h-files, and sometimes the e-file is also included.

Knight The only piece that does not move in a straight line; the two knights on each side jump in an L-shape.

M
Mate Abbreviation for checkmate.

Material All the pieces and pawns on the board, apart from the king.

Middlegame The phase of the game between the opening and the endgame.

N
Notation The method of recording the moves of a game.

O
Open file A file on which there are no pawns of either color.

Opening The first phase of the game; when the pieces are brought into position before the start of any attack.

P
Pawn The footsoldier of the chess board. Each army has eight pawns.

Perpetual check A series of checks that leads to a draw.

Piece In general, a member of the chess army. Sometimes used in the context of a piece meaning a king, queen, bishop, knight, or rook, as opposed to a pawn.

Pin An attack on a piece which, if it should move, leaves a more valuable piece open to capture.

Promotion Where a pawn becomes a queen, knight, rook, or bishop when it reaches the end of the board.

Q
Queen (noun) The most powerful piece on the board. Each army has one queen and she can move in a horizontal, vertical, or diagonal direction.

Queen (verb) To promote a pawn to a queen.

Queen's side The files that are nearest the queen – the a-, b-, and c-files, and sometimes the d-file is also included.

R
Rank A straight row of squares going horizontally from one side of the board to the other.

Rook Each army has two rooks, which resemble castle towers. They move in a straight line along the ranks and files.

S
Sacrifice To give up material in order to fend off an attack or to gain advantage.

Scholar's mate A four-move checkmate, which can occur quite often between beginners.

Score The written record in notation of the moves of a game, usually on a score sheet.

Stalemate A position in which a king is not in check but the player has no legal move. Such a position is a draw.

Strategy The planning of long-term moves in a game rather than short-term tactics and actions.

T
Tactics The art of the double or multiple threat.

Answers

Page 13: Simple notation
White: Queen is on c1
            Bishop is on g2
            Pawn is on d4
Black: King is on e8
            Knight is on b6
            Rook is on h5

Page 14: Pawns
White pawns can capture the knight on d4, the bishop on b4, and the pawn on e5.

Page 16: Bishops
The bishop moves in either of the following orders:
f6, d8, b6, a5, c3, e1, f2, g3
or: f6, d8, b6, f2, g3, e1, c3, a5

Page 17: Knights
The knight jumps in either of the following orders:
d6, f5, g7, e6, d8, f7
or: d6, f7, d8, e6, g7, f5

Page 18: Rooks
The rook moves in the following order:
f5, f3, g3, h3, h7, f7, d7, b7, b4

Page 21: King
1. White's rook moves to h8 to give checkmate
2. White's bishop moves to d5 to give checkmate
3. White's queen moves to c7 to give checkmate

Page 25: Further notation
1. The four moves are written as follows:
bxa3, Nxg1, g5, and Bd6+

Page 27: Opening
1a. Pawn to e4: good move.
b. Pawn to h4: bad move because it puts a pawn on the edge.
c. Knight to h3: not good – you move out a knight (Rule 2) but you put it on the edge.

2a. Bishop to b5: bad move – you've already moved the bishop once.
b. Knight to a3: bad move. Again, you moved out a knight, but put it on the edge.
c. Pawn to d3: good move. It puts a pawn in the center and releases the bishop at c1.

3a. Knight to f3: bad move. You get a knight near the center (Rule 2) but you lose your pawn at e4, which is threatened by the black bishop at b7. Guard your pieces! (Rule 4).
b. Pawn to e5: not good! Only move each piece once (Rule 3).
c. Knight moves to c3: good choice! You get out a new piece (Rule 2) and you also defend your pawn at e4 (Rule 4).

Page 31: Essential techniques
1. White can make the following captures:
Kxe3 (1 point), Kxf3 (3 points), Kxg3 (3 points), bxa6 (3 points), Nxf6 (5 points), Bxg8 (9 points – the best capture)

2. Qxf5 – not good as Black can recapture with a pawn, and White will lose the queen
gxh4 – good move because Black can only recapture a pawn, and White has won a bishop
Rxc7 – an equal exchange as Black can recapture your rook with the black rook on h7
Bxf8 – White wins Black's queen. Black's king will recapture White's bishop but the profit for White is 6 points. This is therefore the best capture for White.

3. The nine safe moves for White are:
Qg1, Kg1, Rc3, Ra1, Na1, Qe1, Ke1, h4, Bb5

4. Rd4 – safe
Bxc7 – not safe
Rd7 – safe-enough
Be5 – safe-enough

Page 32: Attack and defend
1. White can make the following threats:
Bb6 attacking the rook at d8
Rc7 attacking the pawn on b7
Rg1 attacking the queen on g7
Bh4 attacking the rook on d8

2. The six threatening moves are:
Qf7 attacks the bishop at e7
Nf5 also attacks the bishop at e7
Rd5 attacks the queen at c5
c4 attacks the knight at b5
Ne4 attacks the queen at c5
Qf3 attacks the rook at a8
If you found them all, congratulations!

Page 33: Attack and defend (continued)
1. Support: Kg2, Kh2, Rc3
Counterattack: Rc7 attacks the knight at b7, Rc8+ attacks the king at g8
Move: Ng5 moves the knight to a safe-enough square

2. Move: Qe2, Qe1, Qb6
Block: f4
Counterattack: also f4, attacks both the knight at e5 and the bishop at g5; Bd5+ attacks the king at g8

Page 36: Endgame
1. The best move for White is Bd7, as next move the bishop can "mop up" the pawn at b5 and go on to "queen a pawn," ensuring victory.

2. Yes, White should capture the rook and then be recaptured ("swap down"). White will then be able to "queen a pawn" on the h-file.

Page 38: It's a draw!
Rg3. Black's next move has got to be to capture the rook which has the king in check. White can then not move the king – stalemate!

Index

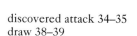

Useful addresses

World Correspondence Chess Federation
1403 Inyo Street 21
Crescent City
California 95531
Tel: 1-707-464-6020
Website www.ewccf.com

FIDE (Fédération Internationale des Échecs)
email address: office@fide.com
Website: www.fide.com

USCF (United States Chess Federation)
PO Box 3967
Crossville
TN 38557
Tel: 931-787-1234
email address: feedback@uschess.org
Website: www.uschess.org

Chess Federation of Canada
356 Ontario Street
Suite 373
Stratford
ON N5A 7X6
Tel: 519-508-2362
email address: info@chess.ca
Website: www.chess.ca

World Chess Hall of Fame
4652 Maryland Avenue
St. Louis
Missouri 63108
Tel: 314-367-9243
email address: info@worldchesshof.com
Website: www.worldchesshof.org

Useful websites

General links:
www.chess.co.uk

Playing chess online:
www.chessclub.com
www.chess.net

Chess chat:
www.chesscenter.com/twic/twic.html
www.chesscafe.com

Kasparov websites:
www.kasparov.com

Chess lessons:
www.chesscorner.com

Mind Sports Olympiad:
www.boardability.com

Chess supplies and products:
www.chessdigest.com
www.chessmate.com

Aficionado "Chess Mentor" learning engine and products:
www.chess.com

Acknowledgments

Special thanks to Caroline Greene, Amanda Rayner, Lee Simmons, and Penny York for editorial assistance; Jacqueline Gooden, Tory Gordon-Harris, Rebecca Johns, and Tassy King for design assistance; Hilary Bird for preparing the index; and Giles Powell-Smith for designing the jacket.

Picture credits
The publisher would like to thank the following for their kind permission to reproduce their photographs: *a* = above; *c* = center; *b* = below; *l* = left; *r* = right; *t* = top.
AKG London: *22tr.* **Allsport:** Chris Cole *38tr*; John Gichigi *40b.* **Michael Basman:** *8cl, 8cr, 40tr.* **Bridgeman Art Library, London/New York:** *12tr, 20tr*; Royal Asiatic Society, London *9tr.* **Camera Press:** *9ca.* **Christie's Images Ltd 1999:** *9cl.* **Mary Evans Picture Library:** *14tr.* **Mark Huba:** *9bl, 41tr, 41cl.* **Hulton Getty:** *24tr.* **Rex Features:** *9cr, 9br*; Tony Kyriacou *41clb.* **Telegraph Colour Library:** Peter Adams *18tr.*

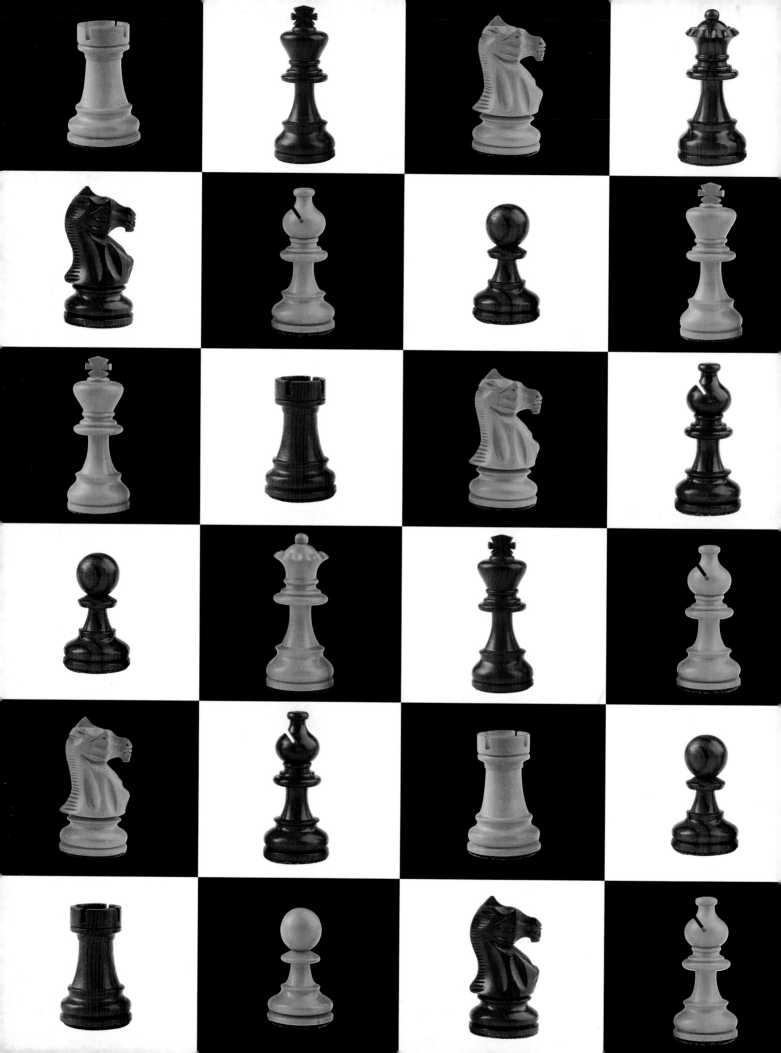

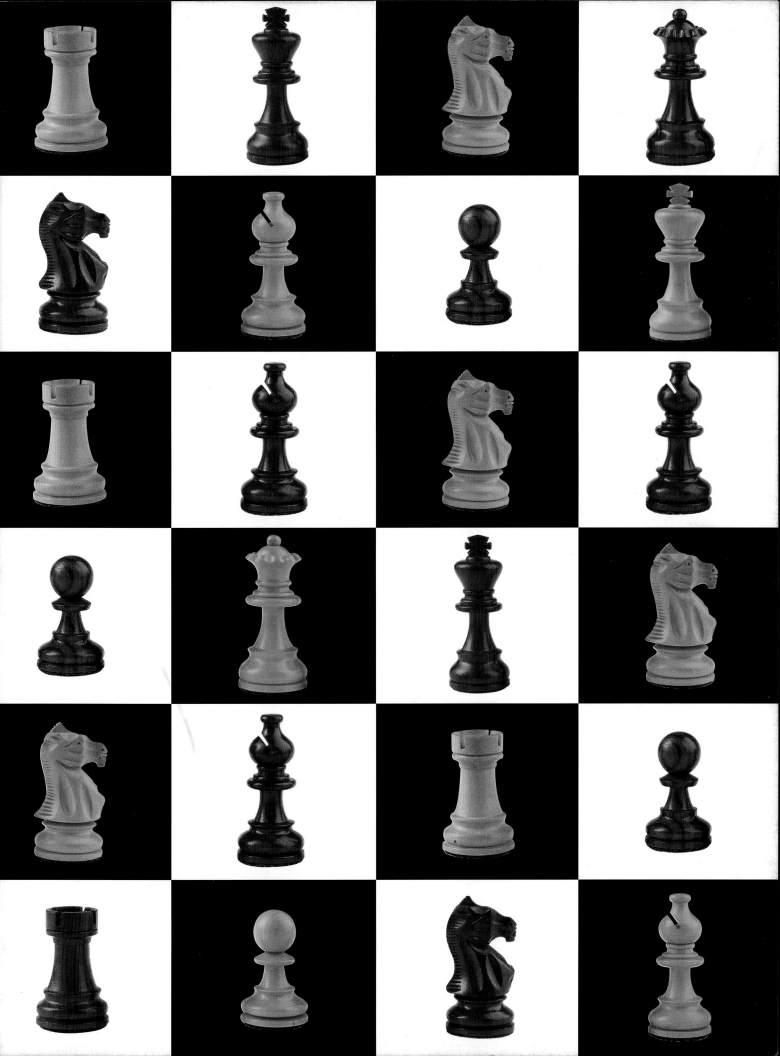